Linux Command Line:
Become a Linux Expert!

**Input/output Redirection, Wildcards,
File Security, Processes Managing,
Shell Programming Advanced Features,
GUI Elements, Useful Linux Commands**

By Matthew Gimson

Disclaimer

While all attempts have been made to verify the information provided in this book, the author does assume any responsibility for errors, omissions, or contrary interpretations of the subject matter contained within. **The information provided in this book is for educational and entertainment purposes only. The reader is responsible for his or her own actions and the author does not accept any responsibilities for any liabilities or damages, real or perceived, resulting from the use of this information.**

The trademarks that are used are without any consent, and the publication of the trademark is without permission or backing by the trademark owner. All trademarks and brands within this book are for clarifying purposes only and are the owned by the owners themselves, not affiliated with this document.

Table of contents

Introduction

In the first part of this book we discussed most of the Linux features, particularly the basics. Linux is the most widely used operating system in production environments, especially on server machines. This means that there is more complexity involved in the use of a Linux operating system. This calls for the need to learn more advanced Linux features.

Most people use Linux commands to perform purely basic tasks. Little do they know that the same commands can be used to perform more complex tasks? A good example of this is the *"cat"* command. Beyond using it to display the file contents of the terminal screen, it can be used for output/input redirection. In this book the Linux advanced features are discussed in detail.

Chapter 1- Definition

There is a lot of information you will learn about Linux after reading this book. In the first part of this book you learned which Linux commands can be run on the terminal. You are now aware of what Linux is, including its origin and the purpose of its development. You are also aware of the people that developed Linux.

The core of Linux is the *"kernel"*, which is the part that communicates directly with the hardware, meaning that it acts as an intermediary between the hardware and the Linux operating system. Those are not the only commands found in Linux. There are more commands that can be used to carry out complex tasks. They will be discussed in this book. You also learned bash scripting tricks. This work will include how to write basic bash scripts.

It is possible to write complex bash scripts on your terminal as well as execute them. You learned how to create Linux shell scripts, although these were basic ones. You can create complex shell scripts that will help you to carry out complex tasks. Most of you might not be able to use the VIM editor. In the first part of this book we used the basic text editor for writing scripts. In this book we will use the VIM editor, which is for experts. It also has extra functionalities, which can also be made using the basic text editor. You have learned about the various Linux Distributions. Use the one you find most comfortable to work with.

Chapter 2- Input/output Redirection

Most processes in Linux require standard input, which is using the keyboard and displaying it on a standard output, a terminal screen. Error messages for these processes are written in standard error, which by default is set to the terminal screen.

You know how to use the *"cat"* command to display the contents of a file on the terminal screen. To demonstrate another use of the command, try the following:

Open the terminal and type *"cat"*. Press the *"Enter"* key. You can then type anything that you want on the terminal and then press the *"Return"* key. Observe what happens.

```
ubuntu@ubuntu-desktop:~$ cat
my name is Kira
my name is Kira
ubuntu@ubuntu-desktop:~$
```

As shown in the figure above, the *"cat"* command can also be used to read input from the standard input, or keyboard. To do this type the command on the terminal without specifying the name of the file. After writing your input, press the "Return" key and this will be displayed on the terminal screen. If you need to end press *"Ctrl + D"*, usually written as "*^D*".

This shows that it is possible to redirect both the input and the output in Linux.

Output Redirection in Linux

It is possible to redirect output in Linux. We use the greater than symbol for this purpose, that is, ">". We will then be able to redirect our output.

Let us create a file named "*names*" containing a list of names.

Open the terminal and type the following command:

cat > names

You can then type the list of names. Make sure that you press the "*Return*" key after each name:

```
ubuntu@ubuntu-desktop:~$ cat > names
john
kira
nicholas
joel
ubuntu@ubuntu-desktop:~$
```

The figure above demonstrates another use of the "*cat*" command.

Now run the following command:

---

cat names

The above command will give the following output:

```
ubuntu@ubuntu-desktop:~$ cat names
john
kira
nicholas
joel
ubuntu@ubuntu-desktop:~$
```

It is clear that the command created a file named *"names"* and then added the names we typed to the file. What happens is that the *"cat"* command reads the input from the standard input and the redirection symbol, that is, *">"* redirects the input to the file *"names"*. Again, to end the input, just press *"Ctrl +D"*.

Appending

To append the standard input to a file in Linux use the symbol ">>". Want to add more names to the file *"names"* you have just created, do the following:

Open the terminal and run the following command:

cat >> names

After typing the above command, press the *"Enter"* key and then type in the list of the names to be added to the file. This is demonstrated in the diagram shown below:

```
ubuntu@ubuntu-desktop:~$ cat >> names
mercy
aladin
clifftone
ubuntu@ubuntu-desktop:~$
```

Open the file to check whether the names have been added to the file. This is demonstrated below:

```
ubuntu@ubuntu-desktop:~$ cat names
john
kira
nicholas
joel
mercy
aladin
clifftone
ubuntu@ubuntu-desktop:~$ █
```

The above figure clearly shows that the new names have been added to the file. It also depicts how clear it is add new contents to an already existing file in Linux. Notice that to end the input simply presses *"Ctrl + D"* as we have been doing.

It is possible to combine the contents of two files into one file in Linux. Create a new file called *"names2"* and add some names to it. This is demonstrated below:

```
ubuntu@ubuntu-desktop:~$ cat > names2
caleb
andrew
ubuntu@ubuntu-desktop:~$ cat names2
caleb
andrew
ubuntu@ubuntu-desktop:~$
```

From the above figure we have created our file and added two names to it. Our aim is to combine the two names in the file with the names in our first file, *"names"* into a single file named *"list"*. Just run the command shown below:

cat names names2 > list

This is demonstrated below:

```
ubuntu@ubuntu-desktop:~$ cat names names2 > list
```

After executing the above command, just check the contents of the file *"list"*. This is demonstrated below:

```
ubuntu@ubuntu-desktop:~$ cat list
john
kira
nicholas
joel
mercy
aladin
clifftone
caleb
andrew
ubuntu@ubuntu-desktop:~$
```

As shown in the figure above we have added the two names in the file "*names2*" to the names in our old file "names". This gives a longer list of names. It is now clear that we can use the redirection symbol ">" to append the contents of one file to another file.

Input Redirection

If you need to redirect the input of a command, use the less than symbol, that is, "<". To sort the input use the "*sort*" command. Let us demonstrate this.

Open the terminal and type in the following command:

sort

Press the enter key and then type in some words starting with different letters of the alphabet. Press the "*Return*" key after each word. Once done, press "*Ctrl + D*" and observe the output. This is demonstrated in the figure shown below:

```
ubuntu@ubuntu-desktop:~$ sort
art
fellow
dog
zebra
water
```

After typing the above words end the input by pressing the key combination above.

The following output should be observed:

```
art
dog
fellow
water
zebra
ubuntu@ubuntu-desktop:~$
```

Beyond using the keyboard to enter the input, it is possible to specify input from certain files using the same symbol. Type the following command:

sort < list

The above command will give the following output:

```
ubuntu@ubuntu-desktop:~$ sort < list
aladin
andrew
caleb
clifftone
joel
john
kira
mercy
nicholas
ubuntu@ubuntu-desktop:~$ 
```

In case you want the sorted contents of a file to be outputted in another file, do the following:

```
ubuntu@ubuntu-desktop:~$ sort <list> file
```

In the command shown in the above figure, we are sorting the contents of the file "*list*" and the output will be outputted in the file "*file*". You can then use the "*cat*" command to view the contents of the file as shown below:

```
ubuntu@ubuntu-desktop:~$ cat file
aladin
andrew
caleb
clifftone
joel
john
kira
mercy
nicholas
ubuntu@ubuntu-desktop:~$
```

Piping

Piping means that the output from a certain process is made the input of another process. In Linux it is represented by the symbol "|", which is the vertical bar.

Consider the command shown below:

who | sort

In the above command we are redirecting the output of the *"who"* command to the *"sort"* command. This is a quick method. If you want to know the number of users currently logged into the system, run the following command:

who | wc −l

Chapter 3- Wildcards in Linux

There are numerous wildcards in Linux. Let us examine them.

The "" wildcard*

It is used to match none or more characters in a specified file. When you want to know the list of files in the current directory whose name start with the letter "*f*", run the following command:

ls f*

The above command is demonstrated in the figure shown below:

```
ubuntu@ubuntu-desktop:~$ ls f*
file   for.sh
ubuntu@ubuntu-desktop:~$ 
```

From the figure shown, it is clear that I only have two files whose name start with the letter "*f*" in the above directory. You can also use the wildcard to know the files whose names end with a certain pattern. For example:

To know all the files whose name end with ...me, run the following command:

ls *me

In my computer, the above command gives the following output:

```
ubuntu@ubuntu-desktop:~$ ls *me
name
ubuntu@ubuntu-desktop:~$ 
```

From the above figure it is very clear that only one file in the directory obeys the pattern specified.

The "?" wildcard

In Linux the above wildcard is used to match exactly one character. Run the following command:

ls f?le

The above command gives the following output in my computer:

```
ubuntu@ubuntu-desktop:~$ ls f?le
file
ubuntu@ubuntu-desktop:~$
```

Getting Help

It is also possible to get help in Linux. If you want to know more about a certain command it is possible to consult from the manual files. To know more about the command "*ls*" run the following command:

man ls

The above command will tell you more about the "*ls*" command the options associated with it. If you want a short description of the command, run the following command:

whatis ls

With the above command the options associated with the command "*ls*" will not be displayed, so use it only when you are not interested with the options.

There may be a time you are not sure how to write a certain command in Linux. To know how use the command "*apropos*" and you will get help. For example:

To know the exact name of the "*copy*" command, type the following:

apropos copy

Chapter 4- File security in Linux

Once you create a long list of your files using the "*ls*" command, the permissions associated with each file are also shown in the output. This is demonstrated below.

After running the command "*ls –l*" on my system, I get the following output:

```
drwxr-xr-x 2 ubuntu ubuntu 4096 2015-03-29 14:07 Desktop
drwxr-xr-x 2 ubuntu ubuntu 4096 2010-04-30 09:24 Documents
drwxr-xr-x 2 ubuntu ubuntu 4096 2010-04-30 09:24 Downloads
-rw-r--r-- 1 ubuntu ubuntu  179 2010-04-30 09:17 examples.desktop
-rw-r--r-- 1 ubuntu ubuntu   60 2015-04-29 06:17 file
-rwxr--r-- 1 ubuntu ubuntu   58 2015-03-31 07:37 for.sh
-rwxr--r-- 1 ubuntu ubuntu   31 2015-04-02 12:32 hello.sh
-rw-r--r-- 1 ubuntu ubuntu   60 2015-04-29 03:56 list
-rwxr--r-- 1 ubuntu ubuntu  143 2015-03-31 02:36 list.sh
drwxr-xr-x 2 ubuntu ubuntu 4096 2010-04-30 09:24 Music
-rw-r--r-- 1 ubuntu ubuntu   95 2015-03-29 12:56 myfile
drwxr-xr-x 2 ubuntu ubuntu 4096 2015-03-30 14:16 myfiles
-rw-r--r-- 1 ubuntu ubuntu  309 2015-03-31 02:51 name
```

The output shows all files in the directory and the permissions associated with each file are also listed.

Manipulating access rights on a file_chmod (change mode)

Only the owner of a file is allowed to change the mode of a file. The following options are associated with the *"chmod"* command:

> u -user
>
> g -group
>
> o - other
>
> a -all
>
> r -read
>
> w -write (and delete)
>
> x -execute (and access directory)
>
> + -add permission
>
> - -delete permission

If you need the read, write and execute permissions for a group or others from the file *"names"*, then run the following command:

chmod go-rwx names

After running the above command the group and others will have no read, write and execute permissions on the file *"names"*. Other permissions on the file will not be affected. To assign a read and write permission to all on the file *"names"*, run the following command:

chmod a+rw names

Chapter 5- Jobs and Processes

A process is a program in execution and it is uniquely identified by a process identifier, or PID. If you want to know the processes which are currently running on your system, together with their status and associated process IDS, run the following command:

ps

On a system the above command outputs the following:

```
ubuntu@ubuntu-desktop:~$ ps
  PID TTY          TIME CMD
 1285 pts/0    00:00:00 bash
 1882 pts/0    00:00:00 ps
ubuntu@ubuntu-desktop:~$ 
```

Linux processes can run either in the foreground or background. They can also be suspended. Once a process starts and is running you will only be able to interact with the command prompt once the process has finished executing. If the process takes a long time to run you will be unable to interact with the command prompt.

It is advisable to run these processes in the background so that you can continue to interact with the command prompt.

Running Processes in the Background

In Linux the use of the "and" symbol, or "&" is used to run processes in the background. If the process takes a long time to run the command prompt will be immediately returned to you. To demonstrate this use the *"sleep"* command, which causes your computer to wait for a number of seconds before continuing with processing?

Type the following command:

sleep 12

After typing press the *"Enter"* key. You will notice the inability to interact with the command prompt until 12 seconds are over.

To run the above process in the background, run it as follows:

sleep 12 &

You will notice that after running the command the prompt will be immediately returned. This is because the long running process is being run in the background. When the background process finishes the user will be notified. The job number and the PID of the process are also returned to the user by the machine.

This is shown below:

```
ubuntu@ubuntu-desktop:~$ sleep 12 &
[1] 1914
ubuntu@ubuntu-desktop:~$ ▮
```

The first number, enclosed in square brackets, is the job number followed by the process ID, or the PID.

You might forget to run a long-running process in the background. This will make it impossible for you to interact with the command prompt. Instead of cancelling the process, it is still possible to remove it from foreground and then run it in the background. This is demonstrated below.

Open the command prompt and run the following command:

sleep 500

The above command will cause the computer to stop execution for a period of 500 seconds. Now that you cannot interact with the prompt, you need to place the process into background. Press "*Ctrl + Z*". This will suspend the process, meaning that it will stop running.

On the terminal, type the following command:

bg

The above command will finally take the process to the background. This is demonstrated below:

```
ubuntu@ubuntu-desktop:~$ sleep 500
^Z[1]    Done                        sleep 12

[2]+  Stopped                        sleep 500
ubuntu@ubuntu-desktop:~$ bg
[2]+ sleep 500 &
ubuntu@ubuntu-desktop:~$
```

After suspending or taking a process into the background, they are entered into a list along with their job id.

To see the process that is currently suspended or running in the background, run the following command:

jobs

On the system the above command gives the following output:

```
ubuntu@ubuntu-desktop:~$ jobs
[2]+  Running                 sleep 500 &
ubuntu@ubuntu-desktop:~$
```

This shows that there is one process running in the background. Notice that the *job id* in the background is also listed in square brackets.

To bring the suspended or process running in the background to the foreground, run the following command:

fg %2

The *job id* of the process running in the background on the system is 2. That explains the 2 used in the above command.

In Linux it is possible to kill certain jobs. A good example of this is an infinite loop. If a process is running in the foreground and you want to kill it, press "*Ctrl + C*". This will kill it as demonstrated below:

Open the terminal and type in the following command:

sleep 200

Press the enter key. You will notice that you can't interact with the command prompt, since the process is a long-running one. Press "*Ctrl* + *C*". Observe what happens. You will have the command prompt back.

This shows that the process has been killed as demonstrated in the figure below:

```
ubuntu@ubuntu-desktop:~$ sleep 200
^C
ubuntu@ubuntu-desktop:~$
```

If you have already suspended the process, or if you are running it in the background, kill it using the following command:

kill %*jobnumber*

The "*jobnumber*" is the job number of the process suspended, or running in the background.

This is demonstrated in the following figure:

```
ubuntu@ubuntu-desktop:~$ sleep 200
^Z[1]    Done                        sleep 500

[2]+  Stopped                        sleep 200
ubuntu@ubuntu-desktop:~$ bg
[2]+ sleep 200 &
ubuntu@ubuntu-desktop:~$ jobs
[2]+  Running                        sleep 200 &
ubuntu@ubuntu-desktop:~$ kill %2
```

The figure shows that after running the process you can take it to the background and kill it. You can then run the *"jobs"* command to check whether it has happened.

To kill a process it is also possible to look for its PID and then use it to complete the task. To the PID of a process, use the command *"ps"*. Make use of this to kill the process. This is demonstrated below:

```
ubuntu@ubuntu-desktop:~$ sleep 200 &
[1] 2049
ubuntu@ubuntu-desktop:~$ ps
  PID TTY          TIME CMD
 1898 pts/0    00:00:00 bash
 2049 pts/0    00:00:00 sleep
 2050 pts/0    00:00:00 ps
ubuntu@ubuntu-desktop:~$ kill 2049
[1]+  Terminated              sleep 200
ubuntu@ubuntu-desktop:~$
```

As shown in the above figure, run a long-running process in the background. Look for its PID and kill it using its PID. After the procedure above, it is good to check whether the process has been killed using the "*ps*" command.

If it has not been killed, force this using the -9 option as shown below:

kill -9 2049

Useful Linux commands

Each user on a Linux system is given a certain amount of space to store files. If this is exceeded, seven days are given to the user to get rid of the excess files. The space is usually located on the hard disk and is always about 100MB.

To know the amount of quota used and the amount that is remaining, run the following command:

quota −v

If you need to know the amount of space being left on the file system, use the "*df*" command.

To know the amount of space that is remaining on the file server, run the following command:

df .

To know the number of kilobytes which have been used by each subdirectory, use the "*du*" command. If you have overused your quarter, you might need to know the subdirectory with the most files.

Navigate to your home directory and run the following command:

du -s *

With the "-s" option, the output will be summarized and with the "*". All the files and directories will be listed.

You might need to use less disk space. To minimize the size of a file to free the disk of some space, run the following command:

ls –l names

After running the above command, keenly note the size of the file names. Mine are shown in the following figure:

```
ubuntu@ubuntu-desktop:~$ ls -l names
-rw-r--r-- 1 ubuntu ubuntu 90 2015-04-29 06:23 names
ubuntu@ubuntu-desktop:~$
```

The size of the file "names" is 90 kilobytes as shown in the figure above. To minimize size, run the following command:

gzip names

You can run the "ls" command. You will notice that the file will be renamed to "namez.gz". Run the following command to check on its current size.

This is demonstrated in the figure shown below:

```
ubuntu@ubuntu-desktop:~$ ls -l names.gz
-rw-r--r-- 1 ubuntu ubuntu 79 2015-04-29 06:23 names.gz
ubuntu@ubuntu-desktop:~$
```

As shown in the figure above, the size of the file has been reduced to 79 kilobytes. To expand the file to its original size, use the *"gunzip"* command as shown below:

```
ubuntu@ubuntu-desktop:~$ gunzip names.gz
ubuntu@ubuntu-desktop:~$ ls -l names
-rw-r--r-- 1 ubuntu ubuntu 90 2015-04-29 06:23 names
ubuntu@ubuntu-desktop:~$
```

Zip the file using the command above. It is tricky when it comes to reading the file without having to undo the compression. It is possible using the *"zcat"* command.

To read the contents of the file *"names"*, run the following command:

zcat names.gz

In case the text scrolls on the screen too fast, pipe it through the *"less"* command as shown below:

zcat science.txt.gz | less

You can also use the *"file"* command to classify the named files according to the type of data that they contain. The data can be pictures, ascii (text) or compressed data.

To classify all the files contained in the current directory, run the following command:

file *

You might also need to compare two files and get the differences between them.

To do this, use the *"diff"* command as shown below:

diff names names2

The above command compares the contents of the files *"names"* and *"names2"* and then outputs the differences between the two files.

The following output will be observed after running the above command:

```
ubuntu@ubuntu-desktop:~$ diff names names2
1,2c1,2
< ubuntu    tty7         2015-04-29 02:51 (:0)
< ubuntu    pts/0        2015-04-29 02:59 (:0.0)
---
> caleb
> andrew
ubuntu@ubuntu-desktop:~$
```

For the lines which begin with the symbol "<", this denotes the first file which is *"names"*, while for the lines beginning with ">", this denotes the second file which is *"names2"*.

With the *"find"* command you can search for files with specification of the desired attributes such as name, size and date. The command also has many options, so you can learn about them from the main pages.

If you want to find the files whose name ends with a *".sh"* extension in the current directory through all the sub-directories and then print on the screen, run the following command:

find . -name "*.sh" –print

You might also need to search for files using the size as the search criteria.

This can be achieved as follows:

find . -size +2M –ls

The above command will search for all files in the current directory whose size is more than 2MB. These files will form the output.

Chapter 6- Advanced Shell Programming

In the first part of this book you were introduced to shell programming and most of its basics were explored. Now we are going to explore the advanced features of shell programming.

Functions in Shell

Shell functions have the following syntax:

function_name ( ) command

They are usually laid out as follows:

function_name() {

commands

}

There is different exit status for functions in a shell. By default they will return an exit status of zero (0). It is good for the programmer to specify the exit status needed. It is also possible to define variables locally within a shell function.

Consider the shell program shown below:

```sh
#!/bin/sh


function_increment() {   # we start by defining the
increment so as to use it

echo $(($1 + $2))


# this will echo the result after addition of the first
and the second parameters

}


# checking for the availability of all the command line
arguments

if [ "$1" "" ] || [ "$2" = "" ] || [ "$3" = "" ]
then
echo USAGE:

echo "   counter initialvalue incrementvalue
finalvalue"

else
c=$1               # renaming variables having clearer
names

value=$2
final=$3
```

while [$c -lt $final]   # if the c is less than final, then loop

do
echo $c

c=$(function_increment $c $value) 2# Calling for increment with c and value as the parameters

done   # the c will be incremented by value

fi

Notice how we have begun by defining our function. We have then added together the first and second parameters being passed into the function. The use of the *"echo"* command will print the result to the standard output. For referencing purposes we use command substitution. This is the line "c=$(function_increment $c $value)".

The parameters *"c"* and *"value"* will be passed into the line where we specified the first and second argument being passed into the function, which is the line "echo $(($1 + $2))". These will then be added together and the result will be printed on the standard output.

Scope of variables

Consider the shell program shown below:

```sh
#!/bin/sh
function_increment() {
  local v=5
  echo "The value is $v within the function\\n"
  echo "\\b\$1 is $1 within the function"
}

v=6
echo "The value is $v before the function"
echo "\$1 is $1 before the function"
echo
echo -e $(function_increment $v)
echo "The value is $v after the function"
echo "\$1 is $1 after the function"
```

We have begun by assigning a value of 5 to our local variable "*v*" and then specified the desired output. We have then called our function using the following line of code:

echo -e $(function_increment $v)

That is what is called a function in shell programming. The use of the "-e" option allows the ability to process the slashes in the correct way. Notice the use of "\\n" as a new line character.

The following output will be observed from the program:

The value is 6 before the function
$1 is 2 before the function
The value is 5 within the function
$1 is 5 within the function
The value is 6 after the function
$1 is 2 after the function

Creating Aliases

Aliases in Linux are used to represent commands. If you need to know all the aliases defined on your machine, run the following command on your terminal:

alias

On the example machine, the above command gave the following result:

```
ubuntu@ubuntu-desktop:~$ alias
alias egrep='egrep --color=auto'
alias fgrep='fgrep --color=auto'
alias grep='grep --color=auto'
alias l='ls -CF'
alias la='ls -A'
alias ll='ls -alF'
alias ls='ls --color=auto'
ubuntu@ubuntu-desktop:~$
```

The above figure shows the aliases defined on this system. All the above are default aliases. You can create aliases as well.

To create aliases, use the following syntax:

alias name='command'
alias name='command argument1 argument2'

The command *"clear"* in Linux is used to clear the terminal screen. To use the letter *"s"* to represent the command, that is, create alias for the command, do the following:

alias s= 'clear"

Run the above command on your terminal. This is demonstrated in the figure shown below:

```
ubuntu@ubuntu-desktop:~$ alias s='clear'
ubuntu@ubuntu-desktop:~$ ls
Desktop          file      list.sh    name      name.sh\  Templates
Documents        for.sh    Music      names     nm.sh     Videos
Downloads        hello.sh  myfile.gz  names2    Pictures
examples.desktop list      myfiles    name.sh   Public
ubuntu@ubuntu-desktop:~$
```

Since I have used the *"ls"* command to see the files in the directory, I need to clear the terminal. Type the letter *"s"* on the terminal and press the enter key. It will clear the terminal.

The command *"date"* in Linux is used to display the current date. Create alias for it. Use letter *"d"* as alias for the same command.

This is demonstrated in the figure shown below:

```
ubuntu@ubuntu-desktop:~$ alias d='date'
ubuntu@ubuntu-desktop:~$ d
Wed Apr 29 11:43:46 MDT 2015
ubuntu@ubuntu-desktop:~$
```

As shown in the above figure, the letter "*d*" is used as alias for the "*date*" command. After typing the letter "*d*" on the terminal, press the "*Enter*" key and the current date is displayed.

Aliases are very important in Linux. If you want to save on typing time then create them. The name for alias should be easy to remember, including the commands that they represent.

You might find the need to delete aliases you have created. This can be achieved as follows:

On this system, I have the following aliases:

```
ubuntu@ubuntu-desktop:~$ alias
alias d='date'
alias egrep='egrep --color=auto'
alias fgrep='fgrep --color=auto'
alias grep='grep --color=auto'
alias l='ls -CF'
alias la='ls -A'
alias ll='ls -alF'
alias ls='ls --color=auto'
alias s='clear'
ubuntu@ubuntu-desktop:~$ █
```

Note the presence of the two aliases that were created previously. To delete the alias "d" representing the *"date"* command, run the following command:

unalias d

This is demonstrated in the figure shown below:

```
ubuntu@ubuntu-desktop:~$ unalias d
ubuntu@ubuntu-desktop:~$ d
d: command not found
ubuntu@ubuntu-desktop:~$
```

As shown in the above figure, after deleting the alias and then trying to use it, the computer states that it is not found.

It is possible to remove more than one alias at once. If you need to remove the aliases "*d*" for "*date*" and "*s*" for "*clear*" the following command should be used:

unalias d s

The above command will delete the two aliases. After running the command you can then run the "*alias*" command to check whether they are still available.

Tilde Expansion in Linux

In most cases Linux users use the tilde (~) symbol to refer to their home directory, while others use the home directory.

To see your home directory file listing run the following command:

ls ~

To view the "*.bashrc*" file located in the home directory, run the following command:

cat ~/.bashrc

ls ~/.bashrc

The first command will open the file on the terminal window. This is demonstrated below:

```
ubuntu@ubuntu-desktop:~$ cat ~/.bashrc
# ~/.bashrc: executed by bash(1) for non-login shells.
# see /usr/share/doc/bash/examples/startup-files (in the package bash-doc)
# for examples

# If not running interactively, don't do anything
[ -z "$PS1" ] && return

# don't put duplicate lines in the history. See bash(1) for more options
# ... or force ignoredups and ignorespace
HISTCONTROL=ignoredups:ignorespace

# append to the history file, don't overwrite it
shopt -s histappend
```

The second command will show the directory where the file is located. This is shown in the following figure:

```
ubuntu@ubuntu-desktop:~$ ls ~/.bashrc
/home/ubuntu/.bashrc
ubuntu@ubuntu-desktop:~$
```

If the prefix for the tilde symbol is a plus (+), this will substitute the "*PWD*" command. If it is preceded by a negative sign, or (-), then the variable "OLTDPWD" is substituted if it had been set.

It is good to note that Linux commands can either be built-in or in an external binary file. To know where a command belongs, we use the "*type*" command.

To know whether the command "*ls*" is built-in, run the following command:

type –a ls

The above command will give the following output:

```
ubuntu@ubuntu-desktop:~$ type -a ls
ls is aliased to `ls --color=auto'
ls is /bin/ls
```

To know whether the *"history"* command is built-in or an external command, run the following command:

type –a history

```
ubuntu@ubuntu-desktop:~$ type -a history
history is a shell builtin
ubuntu@ubuntu-desktop:~$
```

It is worth noting that some commands in Linux can be both built-in and external.

To demonstrate this, run the following commands:

type –a echo

The above command will give the following output:

```
ubuntu@ubuntu-desktop:~$ type -a echo
echo is a shell builtin
echo is /bin/echo
ubuntu@ubuntu-desktop:~$
```

Nested "ifs" in Shell

Nested "*if*" means that it is an "*if*" statement inside another "*if*" statement.

It follows the following structure:

if condition

    then

        if condition

        then

            . . .

            Statement to be executed

        else

            ...

            Stamen to be executed

        fi

    else

        ...

        .....

        Statement to be executed

    Fi

Exit status for commands

After a command executes and terminates either normally or abnormally, it must return an exit status. The exit status is usually an integer value. An exit status of zero (0) means that the command executed successfully. Any other exit status, which can range from 1-255, means that the command failed to execute.

To know the exit status of a previously executed command, use the variable "?", which is a special character in shell.

To determine the exit status run the following command:

echo $?

This will give the exit status of the previously executed command. In the example system it offers the following result:

```
ubuntu@ubuntu-desktop:~$ echo $?
0
ubuntu@ubuntu-desktop:~$
```

The result is a zero (0), meaning that the previously executed command on the system executed successfully.

To demonstrate this practically begins by running the *"ls"* command on your system. Make sure that it runs successfully. On the example system it gives the following result:

```
ubuntu@ubuntu-desktop:~$ ls
Desktop         file        list.sh     name      name.sh\  Templates
Documents       for.sh      Music       names     nm.sh     Videos
Downloads       hello.sh    myfile.gz   names2    Pictures
examples.desktop list       myfiles     name.sh   Public
ubuntu@ubuntu-desktop:~$
```

Since it has run successfully, try to check its status using the special shell character.

Run the following command:

echo $?

The above command should return an exit status of zero (0) since the previous command executed successfully.
This is demonstrated in the figure shown below:

```
ubuntu@ubuntu-desktop:~$ echo $?
0
ubuntu@ubuntu-desktop:~$
```

This time try to run a command that is not recognized and then check the exit status. Run the following command:

ls1

You are very much aware that the above command does not exist in Linux. Running it will result in an error.

In the example system it gives the following result:

```
ubuntu@ubuntu-desktop:~$ ls1
No command 'ls1' found, did you mean:
 Command 'lsh' from package 'lsh-client' (universe)
 Command 'lsw' from package 'dwm-tools' (universe)
 Command 'ls' from package 'coreutils' (main)
ls1: command not found
```

The output shows that the command has not been found. This means that it does not exist in Linux.

To check its exit status, run the usual command, which is shown below:

echo $?

The above command gives the following output on the example system:

```
ubuntu@ubuntu-desktop:~$ echo $?
127
ubuntu@ubuntu-desktop:~$
```

The exit status is not zero (0), meaning that the command did not execute successfully. The returned integer is between 0 and 255 as we initially said. To conclude this, any command whose exit status is not zero did not execute successfully.

Conditional execution in shell

In Linux shell programming it is possible to join two commands, where the execution of the second command will be based on the first.

Logical AND

This takes the following syntax:

1stcommand && 2ndcommand

With this conditional execution, the "2ndcommand" will be executed if and only if the "1stcommand" returned an exit status of zero (0). This means that you should first run the "1stcommand" if the "2ndcommand" runs successfully.

Let us demonstrate this using an example.

In the current directory I have the following file:

```
ubuntu@ubuntu-desktop:~$ ls
Desktop          file      list.sh   name     name.sh\  Templates
Documents        for.sh    Music     names    nm.sh     Videos
Downloads        hello.sh  myfile.gz names2   Pictures
examples.desktop list      myfiles   name.sh  Public
```

Let me try to delete the file named *"file"* and then echo a message afterwards. I run the following command:

rm file && echo "file has been deleted"

The above command will return the following result:

```
ubuntu@ubuntu-desktop:~$ rm file && echo "file has been deleted"
file has been deleted
```

The output clearly shows that the first command ran successfully, followed by the second command. Try to run an incorrect command first to see what happens.

From the list of files in the directory there is no file named "fruits". Try to delete a file with that name and then echo a message afterwards.
Run the following command:

rm fruits && echo "the file has been deleted"

The above command will give the following result:

```
ubuntu@ubuntu-desktop:~$ rm fruits && echo "file has been deleted"
rm: cannot remove 'fruits': No such file or directory
ubuntu@ubuntu-desktop:~$
```

The command returns an error message. This means that the first command had no exit status of zero since it did not run successfully. If it had run successfully we would have the correct result.

Suppose you want to use the "*grep*" command to search for a particular word or name in a file. You can make the use of the logic AND to echo the result. Give the file "*names2*" two names. Search for the name "*caleb*" in the file.

Run the following command:

grep "caleb" names2 && echo "The name was found"

The above command gives the following result:

```
ubuntu@ubuntu-desktop:~$ grep "caleb" names2 && echo "The name was found"
caleb
The name was found
ubuntu@ubuntu-desktop:~$
```

The above figure shows that the first command exited with an exit status of 0, so the second command was run successfully.

Logic OR

It is a Boolean operator. Programmers can make use of this operator to execute a certain command based on another command.

It takes the following syntax:

1stcommand || 2ndcommand

The command "2ndcommand" will be executed if and only if the command "1stcommand" executes unsuccessfully, meaning that it returns a non-zero exit status. In other words, you can run only one of the commands. This means that if the first command runs successfully, the second command will be unsuccessful and vice versa.

Consider the following Linux command:

grep "caleb" names2 || echo "The name was not found"

The above command will output the following:

```
ubuntu@ubuntu-desktop:~$ grep "caleb" names2 || echo "The name was found"
caleb
ubuntu@ubuntu-desktop:~$ 
```

The output shows that the name *"caleb"* was successfully found in the specified file. Notice that the second command was not executed. This is because we can only execute one of the commands.

Consider the example command shown below:

grep "john" names2 || echo "The name was not found"

The above command gives the following output:

```
ubuntu@ubuntu-desktop:~$ grep "john" names2 || echo "The name was found"
The name was found
ubuntu@ubuntu-desktop:~$ 
```

From the output shown above it is very clear that the second was executed. The first command executed unsuccessfully and this led to the execution of the second command. This is because there is no name *"john"* in the specified file.

This can be demonstrated using another example.

Try to delete a certain file from the current directory. The following command should be used:

rm for.sh || echo "file not deleted"

In the directory there is a file named *"for.sh"*. I then try to delete it. Since the first command succeeds, meaning that the file will be deleted, the second command will not be executed. After running the command I get back to the terminal since the operation has been completed.

This is demonstrated in the figure shown below:

What will happen when trying to delete a file that is not present? It is demonstrated using the following example.

Try to delete a file which does not exist in the directory. Run the following command:

rm myfile || echo |file not found"

The above command tries to delete a file which does not exist in the current directory. If the deletion fails the second part of the command should be executed. In the example system the above command gives the following result:

```
ubuntu@ubuntu-desktop:~$ rm myfile || echo "file not found"
rm: cannot remove `myfile': No such file or directory
file not found
ubuntu@ubuntu-desktop:~$
```

The first part of the command ran unsuccessfully, meaning that it had a non-zero exit status. This led to the execution of the second part of the command.

It is also possible to combine the two logical operators into one. Consider the command shown below:

grep "caleb" names2 && echo "name found" || echo "not found"

On this system the above command gives the following output:

```
ubuntu@ubuntu-desktop:~$ grep "caleb" names2 && echo "name found" || echo "not f
ound"
caleb
name found
ubuntu@ubuntu-desktop:~$
```

Notice that only the first two commands have been executed. The last command has not been executed. Try to search for a name which is not available in the specified file.

The command below can be used:

grep "john" names2 && echo "name found" || echo "not found"

The above command gives the following output:

```
ubuntu@ubuntu-desktop:~$ grep "john" names2 && echo "name found" || echo "not fo
und"
not found
ubuntu@ubuntu-desktop:~$
```

It is very clear that the first two parts of the above command have not been executed. The second part of the command will only be executed if the first part of the command returns an exit status of zero (0). This is due to the use of the logical *"AND"* operator.

The last part of the command is executed on its own if and only if the first two parts of the command run unsuccessfully.

Logical Not

This is also a logical operator and it is used for testing whether an expression is true or not.

It takes the following syntax:

! expression

It can also take the following syntax:

[! expression]

You can combine it with the "*if*" statement as shown below:

if test ! condition
               then

1stcommand
2ndcommand
               fi

Or
if [! condition]
               then

    1stcommand
    2ndcommand
               fi

If the expression is false it will return true. Consider the example shown below:

! –f name && exit

After running the above the command prompt will close if the file "*name*" is not found. In this case it doesn't exit since there is a file with the name.

"Continue" statement in shell

This statement is used in shell to resume an iteration of a FOR, WHILE or UNTIL loop enclosing. It takes a very simple syntax:

```
...
while true
do
        [ 1stcondition ] && continue
        Command 1
        Command 2
        [ 2ndcondition ] && break
done
...
```

The statement can also take the following syntax:

```
..
for j in thing
do
        [ condition ] && continue
        Command 1
        Command 2

done
..
...
```

The following is an example of a MYSQL backup script that makes use of the "continue" statement:

```
#!/bin/bash
# A script to backup mysql
# run it while logged in as a root user
# --------------------------------
# Login information
MUSER="admin"                    # MySQL user name
MHOST="192.168.160.1"            # MySQL server ip address
MPASS="password"     # MySQL password
 # date format
NOW=$(date +"%d-%m-%Y")
 # path for the Backupfile
BACKUPPATH=/backup/mysql/$NOW

# create the backup path if it doesn't exist
[ ! -d $BACKUPPATH ] && mkdir -p $BACKUPPATH
 # obtain name lists from the database
DBS="$(/usr/bin/mysql -u $MUSER -h $MHOST -p$MPASS -Bse 'show databases')"

 for database in $DBS
do
```

```
# Backup the name of the file
FILE="${BPATH}/${database}.gz"

# if the name of the database is server or mint,
then skip the backup

[ "$database" == "server" ] && continue
[ "$database" == "mint" ] && continue
# if okay, then we dump the database backup


/usr/bin/mysqldump -u $MUSER -h $MHOST -
p$MPASS $database | /bin/gzip -9 > $FILE

done
```

Exit command

The command has the following syntax:

exit N

Programmers use it to exit for a shell script whose status is "*N*". You can use it to signal either a successful or an unsuccessful termination of a program. If "*N*" is omitted, then the exit status will be that of last command to be executed. You can use this command to end your scripts if an error occurs. Setting "N" to zero (0) means a successful completion of the script.

To demonstrate this, write the following shell script:

```
#!/bin/bash
echo "A test shell script."
# terminate our script with a success message
exit 0
```

I have named this script "*shell.sh*". Note that shell scripts must end with a "*.sh*" extension; otherwise they will not be executed as shell files. Now you can run the script.

Open the terminal and run the following commands:

chmod a+x shell.sh

./shell.sh

The first command will create an executable of the file, which means that it is in the compilation stage. The second command will execute the program. It does so from the executable created by the first command.

After running the above commands you will get the following output:

```
ubuntu@ubuntu-desktop:~$ chmod a+x shell.sh
ubuntu@ubuntu-desktop:~$ ./shell.sh
A test shell script.
```

Now let's check the exit status of the above script.

This can be done by running the following command:

echo $?

The above command will give the following output:

```
ubuntu@ubuntu-desktop:~$ echo $?
0
ubuntu@ubuntu-desktop:~$
```

The exit status of the script is zero (0). This shows that it ran successfully.

Shell yes/no dialog

It is possible to create a dialog which prompts a user to choose either "*yes*" or "*no*" in shell. This is useful when presenting questions to users whose answer is either a "*yes*" or a "*no*". The user is also able to navigate between the "*yes*" and the "*no*" buttons using the "*Tab*" key. Let us demonstrate this using an example program.

Open your editor and write the following shell script:

```
#!/bin/bash
# Yes/No dialog box example
dialog --title "Exit"
--backtitle "A yes/no dialog box example"
--yesno "Are you sure you want to exit the system
\"/tmp/foo.txt\"?" 7 60

 # obtain the exit status
# 0 represents the user hits the [yes] button.
# 1 represents the user hits the [no] button.
# 255 represents the user hits the [Esc] key.
action=$?
```

```
case $action in
    0) echo "You have exited.";;
    1) echo "You have not exited.";;
    255) echo "You pressed the [ESC] key.";;
esac
```

Save the file and then run it. I have given my script the name "exit.sh".

To run it, run the following command:

chmod a+x exit.sh
./exit.sh

After the above commands, a dialog will appear with "yes/no" options.

This is shown below:

A text asking on whether to exit system will also appear.
This is the text that we initially specified:

Password Box

The password box is a box where you can provide a password.

The password that you type is not visible, but appears in a form of dots or asterisks. In other password boxes nothing appears as the user types in the password. This is for the purpose of ensuring the security of your system.

To demonstrate this, write the following shell script:

```
#!/bin/bash
# passwordbox.sh – a shell script that creates a
      password box
# storing the password
d=$(tempfile 2>/dev/null)
 # trap the password
trap "rm -f $d" 0 1 2 5 15
 # receive the entered password
dialog --title "Password Box" \
--clear \
--passwordbox "Key in your password" 10 30 2>
      $data
r=$?
# make your decision
case $r in
  0)
    echo "Password is $(cat $d)";;
  1)
```

```
    echo "You pressed Cancel.";;
  255)
    [ -s $d ] && cat $d || echo "You pressed the Esc
       key.";;
esac
```

Save the script and give it the name *"passwordbox.sh"*. You can then run the script.

Open the terminal and run the following commands:

chmod a+x passwordbox.sh
./passwordbox.sh

After running the above commands, a dialog with a box will appear. This is shown below:

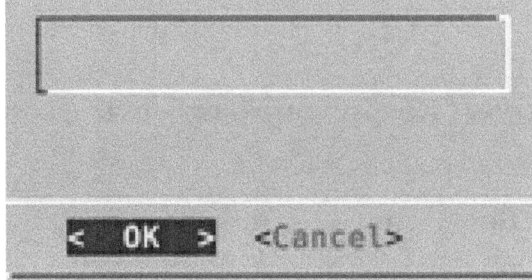

Try to type in your password. You will notice that nothing appears in the password box.

Most people are used to password boxes in which an asterisk
    for each
character typed. It is possible to achieve this in Linux. It is
called the in-secure option.

Write the following shell script:

```
#!/bin/bash
# passwordbox2.sh – a shell script example to read
    user password
# storing the password
d=$(tempfile 2>/dev/null)
 # trapping the password
trap "rm -f $d" 0 1 2 5 15
 # use the in-secure option to get the password
dialog --title "In-secure Password" \
--clear \
--insecure \
--passwordbox "Key in your password" 10 30 2> $d
r=$?
# making a decision
case $r in
 0)
  echo "The Password is $(cat $d)";;
 1)
```

echo "You pressed the Cancel button.";;

255)

[-s $d] && cat $d || echo "You pressed the Esc key.";;

Esac

You can then save the script and give the file a name. I have given my file the name *"passwordbox2.sh"*. Don't forget the *".sh"* extension.

Now run the script by opening the terminal and executing the following commands:

Chmod a+x passwordbox2.sh

./passwordbox2.sh

After executing the above commands, a dialog with a box will appear. Try to key in the password. You will observe the following:

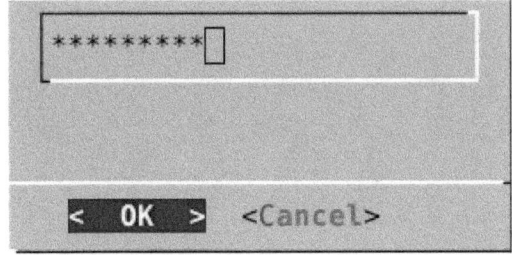

Asterisks will appear for each character that you type.

Progress bar

It is possible to create your own progress bar in shell. You can use it to show the progress of tasks that are being performing such as deleting files, moving files or opening songs. It consists of a meter and a percentage indicating the progress of the task. The percentage keeps on increasing as the task progresses until it becomes 100%.

To demonstrate this write the following shell script:

```
#!/bin/bash
# pbar.sh – a shell script example to create a progress
      bar
# initialize the counter to 0
counter=0
(
# create an infinite "while" loop
while :
do
cat <<EOF
XXX
$counter
Disk copy /dev/dvd to /home/data ( $counter%):
XXX
```

EOF

 # the counter will be incremented in increments of 5 each

((counter+=5))

[$counter -eq 100] && break

 # delay it for a short time of 2 seconds

sleep 2

done

) |

dialog --title "Copying file" --gauge "percentage completion" 7 70 0

You can now save the script. I have named my script *"pbar.sh"*. To run it, run the following commands:

chmod a+x pbar.sh

./pbar.sh

After running the above commands the following output will be observed:

Above is the progress bar. As shown in the figure it indicates the percentage of completion of the task. Mine is at 15% completion. Don't worry if yours shows a different percentage as the speeds of computers will always be different. It might be less or more than the 15%. That is how you can simply create your own a progress bar.

Conclusion

It can be concluded that with Linux a lot can be accomplished. The Linux command line is a very useful tool for programmers. Rather than using it to run the basic commands, there are complex commands which can be run on the Linux command line. The *"cat"* command in Linux is used primarily to display the contents of files on the standard output, which is set to the terminal screen by default.

The command can also be used to redirect both the input and the output. It is possible to use this command to provide input into your system as it can read the input from the standard device, which is the keyboard. You simply need to type the command without specifying a file name and then provide the input. For one to end the input, *"Ctrl +D"* keys should be pressed. It is also possible to use the same command to create file and then enter content into it simultaneously. This shows how powerful and useful command is in Linux.

One can also create aliases to represent most commands in Linux. This is an easy way to remember commands and save time. Linux processes can be suspended or run in the background or foreground. In Linux an exit status of zero (0) signals a successful completion of a process. Any other integer representing an exit status for a process signals an unsuccessful completion. With Linux shell programming you can create very amazing apps. "*If*" statement can be nested, meaning that an "*if*" statement is created within another "*if*" statement. The logical operators can also be used in shell scripts for decision making. You can also create GUIs in shell programming.

Thank you !

Thank you for downloading this book. We hope it was helpful for you in your way to becoming an Expert in Linux Programming. If you need to learn more please find the first book

Linux Command Line FAST and EASY!, which you can download here:

Here is the list of other books form Matthew Gimson:

ANDROID PROGRAMMING: Complete Introduction for Beginners -Step By Step Guide How to Create Your Own Android App Easy!

ANDROID GAME PROGRAMMING: COMPLETE INTRODUCTION FOR BEGINNERS: STEP BY STEP GUIDE HOW TO CREATE YOUR OWN ANDROID APP EASY!

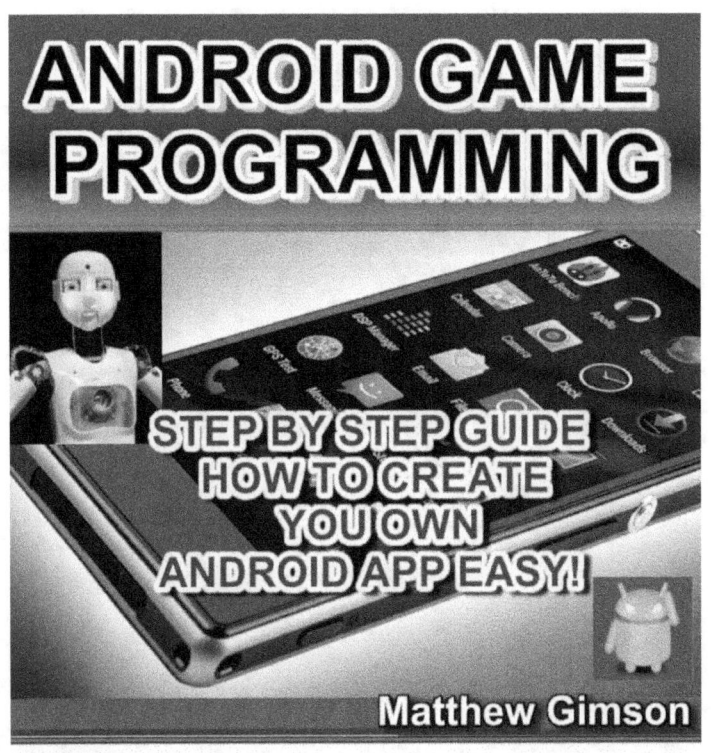

PHP and MySQL Programming for Beginners: A Step by Step Course From Zero to Professional

Python Programming: Getting started FAST With Learning of Python Programming Basics in No Time.

DOCKER: Everything You Need to Know to Master Docker (Docker Containers, Linking Containers, Whalesay Image, Docker Installing on Mac OS X and Windows OS)

Docker: Docker Guide for Production Environment (Programming is Easy Book 8)

Excel VBA Programming: Learn Excel VBA Programming FAST and EASY! (Programming is Easy Book 9)

VAGRANT: Make Your Life Easier With VAGRANT. Master VAGRANT FAST and EASY! (Programming is Easy Book 10)

SCALA PROGRAMMING: Learn Scala Programming FAST and EASY! (Programming is Easy Book 11)

**NODE. JS: Practical Guide for Beginners
(Programming is Easy Book 12)**

IOS 8 APP DEVELOPMENT. Develop Your Own App FAST and EASY!